MW01046640

# Saints Jacinta and Francisco Marto

# Saints Jacinta
# and Francisco Marto
*Shepherds of Fatima*

Written by
**Anne Eileen Heffernan**, FSP
and
**Patricia Edward Jablonski**, FSP

Illustrated by
**Mari Goering**

**P**auline
BOOKS & MEDIA
Boston

Library of Congress Control Number: 2017937017

All rights reserved. No part of this book may be reproduced or transmitted in any form or by any means, electronic or mechanical, including photocopying, recording, or by any information storage and retrieval system, without permission in writing from the publisher.

"P" and PAULINE are registered trademarks of the Daughters of Saint Paul.

Copyright © 2000, Daughters of St. Paul

Published by Pauline Books & Media, 50 Saint Paul's Avenue, Boston, MA 02130-3491

Printed in the U.S.A.

BJFM VSAUSAPEOILL3-1310087 9096-0

www.pauline.org

Pauline Books & Media is the publishing house of the Daughters of Saint Paul, an international congregation of women religious serving the Church with the communications media.

6 7 8 9 10 11                    21 20 19 18 17

*Encounter the Saints Series*

**Blesseds Jacinta and Francisco Marto**
*Shepherds of Fatima*

**Blessed James Alberione**
*Media Apostle*

**Blessed Pier Giorgio Frassati**
*Journey to the Summit*

**Journeys with Mary**
*Apparitions of Our Lady*

**Saint Anthony of Padua**
*Fire and Light*

**Saint Andre Bessette**
*Miracles in Montreal*

**Saint Bernadette Soubirous**
*And Our Lady of Lourdes*

**Saint Catherine Labouré**
*And Our Lady of the Miraculous Medal*

**Saint Clare of Assisi**
*A Light for the World*

**Saint Elizabeth Ann Seton**
*Daughter of America*

**Saint Faustina Kowalska**
*Messenger of Mercy*

**Saint Francis of Assisi**
*Gentle Revolutionary*

**Saint Gianna Beretta Molla**
*The Gift of Life*

Saint Ignatius of Loyola
*For the Greater Glory of God*

Saint Joan of Arc
*God's Soldier*

Saint John Paul II
*Be Not Afraid*

Saint Kateri Tekakwitha
*Courageous Faith*

Saint Martin de Porres
*Humble Healer*

Saint Maximilian Kolbe
*Mary's Knight*

Saint Pio of Pietrelcina
*Rich in Love*

Saint Teresa of Avila
*Joyful in the Lord*

Saint Thérèse of Lisieux
*The Way of Love*

Saint Thomas Aquinas
*Missionary of Truth*

Saint Thomas More
*Courage, Conscience, and the King*

*For even more titles in the
Encounter the Saints series,
visit: www.pauline.org./EncountertheSaints*

# CONTENTS

## 1

## FUN AND FREEDOM

"Wait, Francisco!" six-year-old Jacinta panted. "Wait for me!"

Francisco grinned as he turned back toward his sister. He was almost two years older than Jacinta, and sometimes he was just too quick for her.

"All right," he called over the bleating of their lambs. "But if we don't hurry, we won't catch up with Lucia!"

The day was a perfect one for the two shepherds, the youngest of the eleven children of Peter and Olympia Marto. The sun sparkled over nearby Fatima, a mountain village cradled in the heart of Portugal. Puffy clouds floated overhead as the children's flocks grazed on the slopes.

Francisco lifted his hand to shield his eyes. He squinted and scanned the horizon. "Look! There's Lucia up ahead," he pointed with his staff.

Nine-year-old Lucia dos Santos was more than their cousin. She was their best friend. The three were always together. They would wake up early every morning. Then, before the sun scattered the mists from the valleys, they would be off for the pasture with their flocks. They didn't mind having to get up so early, knowing they'd soon be having fun in the wide-open spaces.

Lucia knew every nook and cranny of the mountains. A hill she especially liked to take her cousins to was called the Cabeço. It was a beautiful spot covered with brightly colored flowers of all kinds. Good pasture-lands could be found there, and in bad weather the children could take shelter in a small cave on the hillside.

The little shepherds carried their lunches with them. They stayed in the fields from morning to evening, returning home at night to join their parents for supper and the family rosary.

As the trio hurried their flocks along, the baaing of the sheep mingled with their prayers—the Our Father, the Hail Mary, the Angel of God. They noticed that if they shouted loud enough, their words would bounce back to them in echoes from the surrounding cliffs. Jacinta soon discovered that the word "Mary" seemed to make the best echo. From then on the tiny shepherdess never tired of shouting "Mary!" to the mountains.

After lunch, they would recite the rosary together. The rosary was a family custom. And customs have to be respected. But the rosary can seem like a very long prayer . . . especially to three young children anxious to have some fun. So one of them—probably Jacinta again—invented a way out. Instead of saying the complete prayers, one of the three would call, "Hail Mary!" and the other two would answer, "Holy Mary!" They would simply end each decade with the two words "Our Father." In this way the rosary was quickly "finished," and they could get back to their games. Often Francisco would play his reed flute while Lucia and Jacinta danced.

The three cousins had very different characters.

As the oldest, Lucia was the leader of the group. She was energetic and cheerful. She was also a very down-to-earth type of person. Her flat nose, rather large mouth, and thick black hair added to her "practical" look.

Jacinta, whose facial features were more delicate than Lucia's, was quick and lively too. But she was also much more sensitive and vain than her older cousin. She liked to have her own way, and if someone said something that offended her, she would easily burst into tears. She could be very possessive at times.

Jacinta loved to dance, and she was really good at it. She also liked taking care of the youngest lambs. She would sit with them in her lap, petting them and kissing them. She even carried the little lambs home on her shoulders at night, so that they wouldn't get tired.

One evening, as they were leading the flocks home, Jacinta dropped behind Lucia and Francisco. "What are you doing?" Lucia asked in surprise as she noticed Jacinta walking in the middle of the sheep. "I want to be like Jesus in that holy picture they gave me," Jacinta explained. "The picture has Jesus right in the middle of all the sheep. And he's carrying one of them in his arms."

Francisco was slower and more thoughtful than Jacinta. His dark eyes were usually full of fun and mischief. Although he had good ideas, he preferred to let Lucia take the lead. He was very sensitive to the feelings of others and liked to let them have their own way—except when it was a matter of right and wrong.

Francisco enjoyed playing with the other village boys. And he never minded when he lost a game. Some of the other boys would take advantage of his good nature, and demand that the game be played over if Francisco had happened to win it. He would give in at once, saying, "All right; it doesn't matter to me."

Francisco loved animals. He used to roll snakes and lizards around with a stick and make them drink sheep's milk that he poured into a hollow of rock. He liked to bring these pets home. But they were never very popular with his mother. Mrs. Marto seemed to always be exclaiming, "Francisco, get that snake out of here!"

Although he could be mischievous, Francisco was kind, both to people and to animals. One day he met a boy who had caught a little bird. "Don't keep him like that," Francisco pleaded. "Can't you see how sad he is? Let him go!"

"I won't," the boy retorted, "not unless you buy him from me." And Francisco did just that—with the little bit of money that he had.

In the countryside, Francisco hunted out the dens of rabbits, foxes and porcupines among the bushes, waded in the clear mountain brooks and sat under chestnut trees, playing his homemade flute and mimicking birdcalls.

He loved to look at the sun, which he called the "lamp of God." How beautiful it was when it rose in the morning, transforming drops of dew into shimmering diamonds, or when it set in the evening and its fiery brilliance blazed from the windowpanes of houses up and down the mountain slopes. What great bursts of light it sent out just before darkness came to swallow up the earth. "No lamp is as beautiful as the Lord's!" Francisco would declare to Lucia and Jacinta.

"I like our Lady's lamp better," Jacinta would answer. (This was her name for the moon.) "It's not hot like our Lord's. It doesn't burn us."

All three children appreciated the natural beauty that surrounded them. But very soon they would see things far more wonderful....

## 2

# "Do Not Be Afraid"

In the spring of 1916, World War I was raging and claiming victims on all its fronts. Many good Portuguese families were in mourning for their loved ones.

One day Francisco, Lucia and Jacinta had eaten their lunch in the little cave on the Cabeço, and, after quickly "saying" the rosary, had started a game. Suddenly a strong gust of wind rattled the trees. The children looked up in surprise. Above the olive orchard at the foot of the hill, they saw a white figure standing in mid-air.

Was it the strange "man in the white sheet" whom Lucia and some other companions had seen in the distance the year before? Yes, it was. But this time the mysterious figure was coming toward them! Its features were those of a handsome teenage boy, about fifteen years old. Its form was transparent and sparkled like crystal. The children's hearts were pounding. They felt happy, amazed and afraid—all at the same time.

As soon as it had come near them, the figure smiled. "Do not be afraid," he said. "I am the Angel of Peace. Pray with me." Then the angel knelt and bowed his head to the ground.

The children dropped to their knees, bowing low until their foreheads touched the ground. They repeated after the angel this prayer: "My God, I believe, I adore, I hope and I love you! I beg pardon for those who do not believe, do not adore, do not hope, and do not love you."

While all three of them saw the angel, only Lucia and Jacinta heard him speak. Francisco could only repeat what he heard his sister and cousin say.

After saying this prayer with the children three times, the angel stood up. "Pray like this," he said. "The Hearts of Jesus and Mary are prepared to listen to your prayers."

Then he disappeared.

Able to think of nothing else but the angel, the children repeated the same prayer, as though forced to do so by an unknown power. They told no one about what had happened.

Months passed. Summer came. One day the three shepherds were playing near the well in Lucia's yard.

Suddenly the same angel appeared beside them.

"What are you doing?" he asked kindly. "Pray, pray much. The Hearts of Jesus and Mary have wonderful plans for you.... Offer prayers and sacrifices to the Most High."

"How can we offer sacrifices?" Lucia was brave enough to ask.

"In every way you can, offer a sacrifice as an act of reparation for the many sins which offend God and as a prayer for the conversion of sinners. In this way you will bring peace to your country. I am the Guardian Angel of Portugal. Above all, accept and bear with patience the sufferings which the Lord will send you."

Kneeling with their foreheads touching the ground, the children prayed. When they finally got up again, Francisco asked, "What did the angel tell you, Lucia?"

"What?" exclaimed Lucia, "Didn't you hear what he said?"

"No. I saw him speaking with you and I heard what you said, but I couldn't hear the angel at all."

The experience had been too overpowering for Lucia to talk about just yet. "Listen, Francisco," she said, "ask me about it tomorrow. Or ask Jacinta."

"Jacinta!" pleaded Francisco. "Tell me what the angel said!"

"I can't. Not now…. Tomorrow!"

That night seemed to drag on forever. Francisco kept waking up, hoping for the break of dawn. Finally it was morning.

"Did you sleep last night?" he asked Lucia as soon as he met her.

"Of course! Didn't you?"

"No. I kept thinking of the angel and of what he said to you."

Then Lucia told him everything, with Francisco interrupting to ask questions. "Who is the Most High? Why is the Lord offended? And why does he suffer so much?"

The answer to this last question impressed the boy more than all the others. It always hurt him to see another person suffer. And now the angel had said that Jesus was suffering because of people's sins!

*Jesus is so good. He loves us so much. If he is suffering, I want to console him*, Francisco decided. He thought about this for a while, then asked more questions.

"Be careful not to tell anyone about this!" Jacinta warned.

"I won't!"

A little later Jacinta added, "After seeing that angel, I don't feel like talking or playing or doing anything at all."

Francisco nodded. "Me neither. But what does it matter? The angel is better than anything. Let's think about him."

Two or three months had gone by when the angel appeared a third time. This time he held a chalice in his hand. Above the chalice, in his other hand, he held a white Host from which drops of Blood were falling into the chalice.

Leaving the Host and the chalice suspended in the air, the angel knelt and bowed his head to the ground. He invited the children to do the same. Then he prayed three times: "O Most Holy Trinity, Father, Son and Holy Spirit, I adore you profoundly. I offer you the most precious Body, Blood, soul and divinity of Jesus Christ, present in all the tabernacles of the world, in reparation for the outrages, sacrileges and indifference by which he is offended. By the infinite merits of the Sacred Heart of Jesus, and of the Immaculate Heart of Mary, I beg the conversion of poor sinners."

Next the angel stood. Taking the miraculous Host, he gave it to Lucia who consumed It. Then he handed the chalice to Jacinta and to Francisco. They drank from it.

"Take," said the angel, "the Body and Blood of Jesus horribly insulted by ungrateful people. Make reparation for their crimes. Console your God."

The angel prostrated himself again, repeated the Most Holy Trinity prayer three more times with the little shepherds, and disappeared forever, leaving the children in ecstasy.

Later, Francisco, who hadn't heard the angel's words, asked, "Lucia, I know the angel gave you Holy Communion, but how about Jacinta and me?"

"That was Communion, too, Francisco. Didn't you see that it was the Blood of Jesus that fell into the chalice from the Host?"

Francisco was satisfied. "I knew that God was in me," he said, "but I didn't know exactly how." Kneeling down with Jacinta, he repeated the prayer of the angel over and over again.

# 3

# THE BEAUTIFUL LADY

On Sunday, May 13, 1917, the cousins went to Mass with their families at Saint Anthony Church, their parish in Fatima. After Mass, they decided to take their sheep to the Cova da Iria.

The Cova is a valley about two miles from Fatima. In this valley Lucia's parents owned a small piece of property where a few holm oaks and olive trees grew. (A holm oak is a type of oak tree whose leaves look like those of the holly plant.)

While the flocks went about feeding upon the best grass, the three friends played games and told stories. Lucia was a great storyteller. She couldn't read, since she had never gone to school, but she had a very good memory. Whenever her mother read stories from the Gospels and the Old Testament, Lucia listened carefully. Later she faithfully repeated the stories to Francisco and Jacinta, who loved to hear them.

After lunch, the trio knelt down to recite the rosary as usual. The fresh spring grass, the shelter of a cave, and the shade of a chestnut tree reminded them of God's power and beauty as they slipped their beads through their fingers. After the rosary, they went back to their games.

The sun shone clearly in the sky, and many field flowers bowed their heads before its hot rays. Suddenly there was an unexpected flash of lightning. The children looked at each other in amazement.

"Maybe a storm's coming up from behind the mountain," suggested Lucia.

Although the horizon was clear, with no clouds in sight, it was better to play safe.

"I think we should go home."

"Yes, let's go!" Jacinta and Francisco agreed.

In a moment the flocks were rounded up and urged down the hillside. Another flash of lightning cut across their path. This time the children were really frightened. They started to run, hoping to arrive home before the storm broke. But when they reached the bottom of the valley, they stopped, as though by command.

A few steps away from them, upon a small green holm oak tree, a beautiful young Lady stood looking down at them.

She was surrounded by a light more dazzling than the sun.

The children's first instinct was to run away, but the Lady reassured them, "Do not be afraid. I do not wish to harm you."

Jacinta and Francisco stared up at her in wonder, while Lucia tried to think of what she should say.

The Lady seemed to be between fifteen to eighteen years old. Her white dress, drawn tight at the neck by a golden cord, fell to her feet. A white mantle bordered with gold covered her head and almost her entire person. In her hands, she held a white rosary with a silver cross. The whole vision shone like crystal in the sun.

The Lady was not standing in mid-air, but resting lightly upon the little holm oak tree, her feet just barely touching its leaves. Her face, of heavenly beauty, was veiled with sadness.

Tenderhearted Francisco was touched at once by her sorrow.

"Where are you from?" Lucia asked.

"I come from heaven."

The Lady's kind voice gave Lucia the courage to continue.

"Please tell us why you have come."

*"Do not be afraid,"* said the beautiful young Lady.

"I have come to ask you children to meet me here at this same hour on the thirteenth of every month, for six months in a row, until October. Then I will tell you who I am and what I wish."

Lucia found it easy to speak to the Lady, whose presence was not overpowering like that of the angel. "If you come from heaven, tell me, will I go there?" she confidently asked.

"Yes," the Lady promised with a look of great love.

"And Jacinta?"

"Jacinta, too."

"And Francisco?"

The eyes of the Lady rested upon the nine-year-old boy, with a thoughtful, motherly gaze. "Yes, certainly he too will come. But first he will have to pray many, many rosaries."

Encouraged by the Lady's goodness, Lucia asked about two little girls who had died recently. From the Lady's reply, Lucia understood that one was in heaven and the other in purgatory. Then the young Lady continued, "Will you offer yourselves to God, ready to make sacrifices and to accept willingly all the sufferings he will send you, in order to make reparation for the sins with which the Divine Majesty is offended and to obtain the conversion of sinners?"

Lucia answered for the three of them, "Yes, we want to!"

The Lady showed her approval with a lovely smile. Then she added, "You will have to suffer much, but the grace of God will assist and comfort you always."

Next, opening her hands, which had been joined, she let a ray of mysterious light fall upon the children. The light seemed to enter right into their hearts and souls. Somehow they knew that the light was God. In fact, they felt embraced by God. Lucia, Jacinta and Francisco fell to their knees. In their hearts they heard the words of this prayer, which they repeated with great love: *Most Holy Trinity, I adore you! My God, my God, I love you in the Most Blessed Sacrament!*

The Lady had one more recommendation: "Say the rosary every day, to obtain peace for the world." Then silently she rose from the treetop and moved off toward the east. The children watched in wonder as the vision slowly faded away.

While the appearance of the angel had left the children unable to speak—often for a few hours—the vision of the Lady had filled them with such peace and joy that they began to talk at once. Francisco, again, had not heard the vision's words, but Lucia immediately told him everything. When he heard that he would go to heaven after he had said many rosaries, he cried excitedly, "Oh, my Lady! I'll say as many rosaries as you want!"

And he would keep his promise.

## 4

# JACINTA'S "BETRAYAL"

After what they had seen, Lucia, Jacinta and Francisco no longer felt like playing. The girls talked about the Lady all afternoon while Francisco listened silently, lost in thought. Many rosaries? Of course, he would say many, if this was what God and the beautiful Lady wanted him to do.

Lucia, who had been teased so much about "the man in the sheet," decided that it was best for them not to talk about what had happened. No one would believe them anyway.

At dusk, they started home. Jacinta skipped along in excitement. Every once in a while she broke the silence by bursting out, "What a beautiful Lady!"

"I bet you'll tell someone about her right away," Lucia said in a worried voice.

"Oh, no!" Jacinta promised. "We won't say a word, will we Francisco?"

"No," agreed her brother. "We won't."

Jacinta had good intentions, but she just couldn't keep the wonderful news to herself. The secret just had to come out. . . . And it did! As soon as Jacinta saw her mother, she threw herself into her arms. "Mama," she cried, "today up at the Cova da Iria I saw the Blessed Mother!"

"What are you saying?" Mrs. Marto asked in astonishment. "Do you think you're so holy as to deserve to see the Virgin?"

"But I saw her! I really did!" Jacinta insisted. "And Francisco and I are going to say the rosary every day. The Lady told us to. And she even promised to take us to heaven!"

Francisco looked at his little sister in horror. She had betrayed their secret. Now what could he do? It was too late to try to make her keep quiet.

At supper that night Mrs. Marto had Jacinta tell her strange story to the whole family. Francisco, true to his promise, kept silent. He only nodded when he was asked if what Jacinta said was true.

Mrs. Marto didn't believe the story. She told it to Lucia's mother, who became very upset about the whole thing. Mrs. dos Santos thought that the three children were lying. The sufferings of Lucia, Francisco and Jacinta were about to begin.

June 13 finally came.

At the appointed hour, the three young shepherds were kneeling at the Cova da Iria, saying the rosary. Ever since the Lady had appeared to them, they had prayed the complete rosary, saying all of the Our Fathers and Hail Marys.

About fifty people had come, out of curiosity, and were whispering among themselves nearby.

Suddenly the children saw lightning. They immediately ran toward the three-foot holm oak above which the Lady had appeared the first time. Yes, she was there, standing in the same spot and surrounded by the same brilliant light!

"What do you wish?" Lucia asked.

"I wish you to come here on the thirteenth of next month, and to recite the rosary every day. After each one of the mysteries, my children, I want you to pray like this: *O my Jesus, forgive us our sins, save us from the fires of hell. Lead all souls to heaven, especially those most in need of your mercy.* I also want you to learn how to read and write. Later I will tell you what else I desire."

Lucia then asked for the cure of a sick person.

"Tell him to lead a better life and he will get well within the year," answered the Lady. Next she confided a secret to the children, telling them not to reveal it to anyone.

Many people tried to guess what the secret was. But only in 1927, after being told to do so by Jesus, did Lucia reveal a part of it.

Lucia had told the Lady, "I would like to ask you to bring all three of us to heaven."

"Yes," the Lady had answered. "I will come for Francisco and Jacinta very soon! You, however, must remain here on earth a longer time. Jesus wants to use you to make my Immaculate Heart better known and loved."

"Then I'll be all alone?" Lucia had asked sadly.

"No, my daughter. I will never abandon you. My Immaculate Heart will be your refuge and the way which will lead you to God."

In pronouncing these last words, the Blessed Virgin had opened her hands and let the penetrating light shine upon the children again. They had seen themselves in the light. Jacinta and Francisco seemed to be in the part of the light that rose toward heaven and Lucia in the part that shone on the earth. A heart encircled with piercing thorns had also suddenly appeared in the Lady's hand. The children understood that it was Mary's Immaculate Heart. But what did it all mean?

5

# TRIALS

"Lucia, did the Lady dance on top of the tree?" someone in the crowd taunted as the three shepherds headed back to the village.

"Jacinta, why are you so quiet? Tell us the secret!" a woman cackled. "And you, Francisco, are you a saint yet?"

The insults and ridicule were painful, but the lack of reverence toward the Lady was what hurt the children the most. Only when they were together by themselves could they talk about what they had seen.

"Why did our Lady stand with a heart in her hand, and shine that great light of God on the world, Lucia?" Francisco asked. "You were standing in the light that came down upon the earth. Jacinta and I were in the light that was going up toward heaven."

"That's because Jacinta and you will go to heaven soon, while I'll stay on earth for a while," explained Lucia. "The heart the Virgin showed us was her Immaculate Heart, which suffers when people offend God."

"How many years do you think you'll stay on earth?" Francisco pressed.

"I don't know, but I think I'll be here for many years."

"Did the Virgin tell you that?"

"No. I saw it in the light which she was shining right into us."

"Yes," nodded Jacinta, who had been listening attentively. "I saw the same thing."

The children's hamlet of Aljustrel, just outside that of Fatima, was a tiny one where everyone knew everyone else's business. Some of the village women couldn't stand the thought of being left out of the Virgin Mary's secret. One day, a few of them, dressed in their Sunday best and sporting gold jewelry, came to visit the Marto family. One of them showed her bracelets and necklace to Jacinta. "Do you like these?" she asked with a smile.

"Oh, yes," replied Jacinta honestly.

"Would you like to have them?"

"Of course!" replied the seven-year-old.

"Then tell us your secret!" exclaimed the woman, taking off the jewelry and holding it out toward Jacinta.

The little girl was shocked. "Don't!" she exclaimed. "Please don't! I can't tell you anything! I couldn't tell you the secret if you gave me the whole world!"

Toward the end of June, Father Manuel Ferreira, their pastor, sent for Mrs. dos Santos, saying that he wanted to see her together with Lucia.

"Finally!" sighed Mrs. dos Santos, in relief. "Father will drive these crazy ideas out of Lucia's head!"

"Listen," she warned Lucia, "tomorrow after Mass we're going to see the pastor. Let him punish you. Let him do whatever he wishes. I'll be happy, as long as he gets you to confess that you've lied."

Lucia kept silent. But as soon as she had the chance, she warned Francisco and Jacinta.

"We're going, too," they replied. "Father Ferreira has also asked our mother to bring us to the rectory."

The next day, the priest carefully questioned the children. He never threatened them with punishment, but he did try to make them contradict each other—all without success.

The secret the children had been given by the Virgin posed a problem. Because they couldn't reveal it to him, the priest felt that they weren't being completely open with him. "It doesn't seem to me that this comes from heaven," he told Lucia's mother. "When the Lord reveals himself to souls, he usually commands them to tell everything to their confessors or pastors. Lucia, instead, closes herself up in silence. It can be a trick of the devil. The future will reveal the truth."

A trick of the devil? This possibility really disturbed Lucia. It bothered her so much that she even had a nightmare about it. She began to ask herself if it wouldn't be better to say that she hadn't seen the vision after all. This would end everything and leave her family in peace.

But when she mentioned the idea to her cousins, Francisco was horrified. "Don't do it, Lucia! You'd be telling a lie, and a lie is a sin."

"All right," Lucia agreed, "I won't. But I'm not going to the Cova da Iria anymore!"

"What? How can you say that!" exclaimed Francisco. "Didn't the Lady tell us that we'd have to suffer a lot in order to make up for sins? Why are you so sad? We

*"I'm not going to the Cova da Iria anymore!"*

can offer this suffering to God for sinners. Let's be happy!"

Lucia understood all this. But she felt confused. She wanted to see the beautiful Lady again, but she didn't feel that she could bear more punishment and insults. She began avoiding Jacinta and Francisco. She would hide when they looked for her and not answer when they called her. What else could she do?

# 6

# July 13

The night of July 12, 1907 found all of Aljustrel in an uproar. In the streets, at the corners, and in the houses everyone was talking about the apparitions. An echo of all this reached Lucia. She wanted so much to see the heavenly Lady again. But what if all this *was* the work of the devil? Lucia shuddered at the thought. Stepping out into the moonlit street, she headed for her cousins' house.

In the old courtyard, Francisco and Jacinta happily ran to meet her.

"Lucia, are you coming with us tomorrow?" Francisco asked hopefully.

"No, I'm not coming. I've told you already that I'm never going to the Cova again!"

"But it can't be the work of the devil!" exclaimed Francisco. "God is already so sad because of the sins people commit. If you don't come to the Cova da Iria, he'll be even sadder. Please come!"

"No. I can't!"

At that point, Jacinta burst into tears.

Lucia walked off, calling over her shoulder, "If the Lady asks for me tomorrow, tell her I stayed away because I'm afraid she might be a devil."

Francisco and Jacinta hardly slept that night. All they could do was cry and pray that the Blessed Mother would make Lucia change her mind.

The next morning, July 13, an "irresistible force" unexpectedly urged Lucia to go back to her cousins' house. Was it the Virgin, who had heard the prayers of Francisco and Jacinta? We can't know for sure, but Lucia did find her cousins kneeling in their room crying and praying.

"How come you're still here?" she asked. "Why didn't you go to the Cova? It's late!"

"We were afraid to go without you," sniffled Jacinta.

"Well, I'm here now, aren't I?" Lucia replied. "Let's hurry!"

It was a hot and muggy day and the sun was merciless. A large crowd had already gathered by the time the children reached the Cova da Iria. There were so many people, in fact, that they had difficulty making their way to the holm oak tree.

All eyes were fixed upon them. At the sound of the noonday bells, the Lady returned, surrounded by a halo of light. But this time, Lucia didn't have the courage to speak to her.

"Come on, Lucia, speak!" Jacinta urged. "Don't you see that the Lady's already here and wants to talk to you?"

Overcoming her fear, Lucia asked, "What do you wish?"

The Lady repeated the same requests she had made before, and at Lucia's begging, she added that she would reveal her name in October, and that she would also work a miracle then. She added, "Sacrifice yourselves for sinners and say often, but especially when making a sacrifice, *O my Jesus, it is for love of you, in reparation for the offenses committed against the Immaculate Heart of Mary, and for the conversion of sinners.*"

But the conversation was not ended. At a certain point, the three children grew pale and trembled. Lucia suddenly screamed. The crowd, which could see nothing but the children's expressions, shuddered with fear.

At the end of the vision, the children remained deep in their thoughts. The spectators, who had seen a white cloud, which dimmed the brightness of the sun as it descended upon the holm oak, understood that the apparition was over. The sun became bright again. The people crowded around the three children and badgered them with questions.

Lucia made every effort to answer them as best as she could. But then the questions began to touch upon the secret the Lady had given them.

"Why were you so sad?" a man asked.

"Why did you scream and tremble?" called out a woman.

The children kept silent. The Blessed Virgin had forbidden them to tell.

The secret is known now in part, because Lucia was later permitted to reveal it.

The Virgin had shown the children a terrifying vision of hell—an ocean of fire. Buried in the flames had been ugly devils, which looked like beasts. These were as transparent as glowing coals of fire. The children had also seen human forms, and had heard screams of pain and desperation that made them tremble with fear.

The three children had looked toward the Virgin for comfort. The Lady had talked to them lovingly and sadly. "You have seen hell, where the souls of poor, unrepentant sinners go," she explained. "To save them, God wants to establish devotion to my Immaculate Heart. If what I tell you will be done, many souls will be saved and there will be peace. But if it is not done, if people do not stop offending God, God's justice will show itself with new and more serious punishments.

"The present war [this was World War I] is about to end. But if people do not stop offending God, not many years will pass by before another and worse war will break out. When you will see the night lit up by an unknown light, that will be the sign God will give you that the world is about to be punished through war, famine, and persecutions against the Church and the Holy Father.

"I come to ask that the world be consecrated to my Immaculate Heart, and that Holy Communion be received in reparation on the first Saturday of every month. If my wishes are fulfilled, I promise that Russia will be converted and there will be peace.

"If the people do not do as I ask, teachings that are disrespectful to God will spread many errors in the world, starting wars and persecutions against the Church. Many good people will be martyred, and the Holy Father will have much to suffer. Many nations will be destroyed. Remember, do not tell this to anyone except Francisco."

As usual, Francisco had seen the Lady, but had not heard her.

Finally, the children saw a vision of an angel calling for penance. Then they saw a bishop dressed in white climbing a steep mountain in a ruined city. They thought he was the Pope. When he reached the mountain top, some soldiers shot and killed him.

We can interpret the secret as referring to things that happened in the last century, especially wars and the sufferings of the Popes and all those who have tried to live and preach Jesus' Gospel. The secret means that God and the Blessed Mother wish us to pray and do penance for ourselves and for others, so that everyone may stop offending God and begin to live in love and mercy—as Jesus has taught us to.

# 7

# FRANCISCO'S MISSION

The same ray of sunlight can have different effects. Passing through an odd-shaped piece of glass, it breaks up into a thousand bright colors. Falling directly on a white wall, it can make that wall as blinding as snow. When passing through a hand or a leaf, sunlight makes the object seem to glow from within.

In the same way, Francisco, Jacinta and Lucia responded differently to the same apparitions. Lucia was to spread devotion to the Immaculate Heart of Mary. Jacinta was to make reparation for sinners. And Francisco? He would try to console God.

"I liked the angel very much," Francisco explained to Lucia and Jacinta, "and I enjoyed seeing the Blessed Virgin even more. But what I loved the most was seeing God in that great light."

He had felt so powerfully attracted to God that he couldn't help thinking of him from then on. The boy who had once refused to say his night prayers now found prayer as natural as breathing.

"I love God very much," Francisco continued, "but Jesus is so sad because of so many sins! If we want to comfort Jesus, we must never sin."

One day Lucia asked him, "Francisco, which do you like most: to console God or to convert sinners so they won't go to hell?"

"I want to console God," Francisco answered right away. "Didn't you notice how the Virgin became sad when she said that people shouldn't offend God, who is already so much offended? I want to console God first, and then convert people so that they won't offend him anymore."

During those summer months while the sheep grazed in the fields, Francisco kept thinking about their vision of God. "Lucia," he confided, "All three of us were inside that great light which is God, but we didn't burn. What's God like? I feel bad that he's so sad!"

While Lucia and Jacinta played, Francisco walked up and down in silence. Whenever they asked what he was doing, Francisco would respond by raising his arm to show that he was saying the rosary.

"Come to play with us now," Lucia would say. "We can pray together later."

Francisco's answer was always the same. "I'll pray now and later, too. Don't you remember what the Blessed Mother said? I have to say many rosaries!"

Francisco often wandered off on his own. Later Jacinta and Lucia would find him praying silently behind a low wall or a bush.

"Why don't you call us to come and pray with you?" Jacinta would ask.

"Because I like to pray by myself so that I can think about God. He's so sad because of people's sins."

One day, the girls couldn't find Francisco anywhere. Lucia was really getting worried. She finally found him crouched beside a stone wall, his forehead almost touching the ground. He didn't answer when she called. She had to shake him until he came to himself again.

"Were you praying?" asked Lucia.

"Yes. I began with the prayers of the angel, and then I stopped to think."

"Didn't you hear Jacinta and me calling you?"

"No, I didn't hear anything. I was thinking about God."

"Come on, let's go find Jacinta. She's crying because she thinks you're lost."

Francisco wanted to stay and think more about God, but going back with Lucia was his chance to make a sacrifice. *I can give up what I'd really like to do and offer this sacrifice to console God*, he thought.

"Okay," Francisco agreed. "Let's go!"

# 8

# GENEROUS HEARTS

The three little shepherds had generous hearts and great goals: "To convert sinners, to console the Lord, and to make reparation to the Immaculate Heart of Mary."

One day, on their way to the pasture, they met some poor children who lived on donations that people gave them. The shepherds had their lunch with them, but they knew for certain that the other children were hungry. Jacinta had an idea: "Why don't we give our lunch to those poor children? We can offer this act of love as a sacrifice for the conversion of sinners."

"Yes, let's do it," agreed Lucia and Francisco.

They gave their lunch to the children that day and every other day that they met them. Because of this, Lucia, Francisco and Jacinta ended up fasting practically every day. Late in the afternoon, when they were feeling really hungry, they would try eating roots, bitter herbs, and even acorns from holm oak trees.

On one of their usual fast days, when Francisco was picking acorns in a holm oak tree, Jacinta suggested, "Let's eat the acorns of the oaks, instead!"

"But those are more bitter!" protested Francisco.

"That's why I want to eat them," Jacinta insisted. "We'll convert more sinners by making a bigger sacrifice!"

Lucia and Francisco followed her example.

One day Lucia's godmother had prepared a delicious sweet drink called hydromel, made of honey and water. She offered a glass of it to Francisco. He passed it to Jacinta, saying, "You and Lucia drink first."

Then, very quietly, Francisco left the house. Jacinta and Lucia went searching for him. They found him sitting by the well in Lucia's yard.

"Francisco, why didn't you take a drink?" Lucia asked. "Godmother has been looking all over for you!"

The boy's face reddened. "Because," he answered, "as I took the glass in my hand, I got the idea of making a sacrifice to console the Lord, and so I decided to give up the drink."

Another day while the three children were playing near the well, Mrs. Marto brought them some fresh grapes. As they were about to eat them, they seemed to hear a voice suggesting that they offer the grapes as a sacrifice. They waited until Mrs. Marto had left. Then they excitedly took the cluster to some poor friends.

Another time the children were given a basket of juicy figs. Just as they were about to take the first bite, Jacinta put her fig down. "We haven't made any sacrifices yet today," she said simply. "Maybe we can give these up." Lucia and Francisco nodded in agreement.

*I love you, God*, Jacinta whispered in her heart, *and I want everyone to love you too.*

# 9

# PRISONERS

The morning of Monday, August 13, 1917, found many cars speeding toward Fatima. The automobile of Arturo de Santos, the mayor of the nearby town of Ourem, was one of them. The mayor stopped at Father Ferreira's house, and asked him to call the three cousins. Mayor de Santos had already questioned Lucia two days before, and had been very upset when she refused to reveal the Lady's secret.

The three shepherds arrived, and answered the mayor's questions—which seemed quite friendly. "I'd also like to go to the Cova, today," he told them.

*Perhaps the Virgin has given the mayor a special grace to make him so friendly*, Lucia thought.

"Come along," Mayor de Santos invited. "I'll drive you there in my car."

Back then, cars were luxuries that only the rich could afford. Coming from poor village families, the children had never ridden in one before! Excited about the opportunity, Lucia, Francisco and Jacinta eagerly scrambled in.

But when they reached a fork in the road, the cousins realized that the car was turning toward the mayor's town, Ourem, instead of the Cova.

"This isn't right!" Lucia burst out. "The Cova da Iria is in the other direction."

"I know, I know," Mayor de Santos replied. "But first we must go to the pastor of Ourem, who wants to see you. Then we'll return to the Cova. We'll still be there in plenty of time to see the Lady. Don't worry."

When they arrived in Ourem, the mayor didn't take them directly to the pastor, even though the children asked him to.

"First you must have lunch," he announced.

The hour for their meeting with the Lady came and went. The children felt miserable. Their only consolation was the thought that they would be allowed to go home soon.

But returning home wasn't part of the plan. The mayor of Ourem hadn't given the children a ride for the fun of it. He intended not only to keep them away from the Cova, but also to learn their secret.

He questioned them for hours, but they wouldn't tell him anything that they had been forbidden to reveal.

Was it possible that a mayor had to give in to three shepherds? This was too much. . . . "You're under arrest!" he finally sputtered, as he slammed the door, locking them in the room. "If you want to get out, you'll decide to talk. Otherwise it will be just too bad for you."

Lucia, Francisco and Jacinta remained locked up all night. They must have encouraged one another by remembering the words of the angel: "Accept with submission the sufferings which the Lord will send you." How many times they must have repeated the prayer: "O my Jesus, it is for love of you, in reparation for the offenses committed against the Immaculate Heart of Mary, and for the conversion of poor sinners"!

The next morning they were brought back to Mayor de Santos' office. This time he tried to win their confidence by offering them gold coins. Lucia spoke first, then Francisco and Jacinta. All three children told him everything that they were free to say about the apparitions. All three of them insisted that they couldn't reveal the secret, because the Virgin had commanded them not to tell it to anyone.

This time the angry mayor had them thrown into the town prison.

Jacinta started to cry. She wanted to see her parents again.

"Don't cry, Jacinta," Francisco said quietly, putting his arm around his little sister. "We can offer this to Jesus for sinners. The worse thing would be if the Lady never came back again. That's what would really make me feel bad. But if she didn't come back, I'd offer it for sinners too." Lifting his eyes and hands to heaven, he prayed, "Jesus, it is for love of you and for the conversion of sinners."

"And in reparation for the offenses against the Immaculate Heart of Mary," Jacinta added in a shaky voice.

The scene moved some of the hardened criminals to tears. "Just tell them the secret and they'll let you go," one of them advised.

"No! I'd rather die!" Jacinta exclaimed.

It was getting dark when the children remembered that they'd forgotten to say the rosary. Jacinta took off the medal that she wore around her neck and asked one of the prisoners to hang it on a nail in the wall. The three of them then knelt down to pray the rosary. The other prisoners knelt with them. Soon the gruff voices of the men joined in prayer with the silvery voices of the young shepherds.

At one point, Francisco noticed that one of the kneeling men hadn't taken off his hat.

"If you want to pray," he whispered kindly, "you should take off your hat."

The man immediately removed his hat and handed it to Francisco, who went over to the bench and laid it on top of his own. They continued the rosary together.

## 10

# "WE'LL USE FORCE!"

Not long after the children had finished praying, the jailer arrived on the scene. "Come with me!" he bellowed.

The three were taken to the mayor's office and interrogated once again. But once again the mayor failed to obtain the secret.

"If they won't obey when we treat them well, we'll use force!" he shouted in frustration.

He called in a guard. "Take them into the next room and prepare a pot of boiling oil," he commanded. "We'll fry them like fish!"

Jacinta, Francisco and Lucia were locked in the adjoining room. After some time passed, Jacinta was taken out.

"If you won't speak, you'll be the first to be fried," the mayor threatened. "Come with me!"

Jacinta had finally stopped crying. The thought that soon she would be with her Lady forever made her happy. As usual, she refused to answer any questions.

In the meantime, Francisco whispered to Lucia, "If they kill us, as they say they will, we'll soon be in heaven!" Then he thought of Jacinta. "May God help Jacinta not to be afraid," he said. "I'm going to say a Hail Mary for her."

He was still praying when the door banged open again.

"She's already dead!" the mayor announced. "Now it's your turn! Out with the secret!"

"No! I can't tell it to anyone!"

"You can't tell it? We'll see about that! Come here!" he shouted, roughly grasping Francisco by the arm.

Like Jacinta, Francisco refused to answer questions about the secret. He was soon shut up in another room, where he found Jacinta waiting. She hadn't been harmed. The brother and sister had never been so happy to see each other!

Lucia, the last to be questioned, was convinced that the mayor was serious about putting them to death. But she wasn't afraid. She prayed to the Blessed Mother to make her strong. And her prayers were answered. Unable to force Lucia to reveal the secret either, the mayor had her put in the same room with her cousins.

*"She's already dead! Now it's your turn!"*

The next morning, after one final attempt to force them to reveal the secret, Mayor de Santos was obliged to take the three brave children back to the rectory at Fatima.

How relieved their families were to have them home after two long, anxious nights!

What had happened, meanwhile, at the Cova da Iria?

On August 13, about 18,000 people had arrived there to wait for the hour of the apparition. Cars, carts, bicycles and horses jammed the field.

The hot sun blazed down on the crowd. Time dragged on. It was close to noon. Rosaries had been recited, and hymns sung, but there was still no sign of the little shepherds. What was going on? Had the children had an accident? Was the whole thing a hoax?

Suddenly a rumor rushed through the restless crowd. The mayor of Ourem had taken the children away with him!

Indignation, anger and threats rose up on all sides. The more excitable members of the crowd wanted to storm the mayor's residence and take the children by force.

All at once the rumble of thunder was heard. All heads turned toward the little holm oak tree. Lightning flashed, and a beautiful white cloud appeared above the tree.

"Look! Look!" someone shouted. "It's a sign from our Lady!" After hovering over the tree for about ten minutes, the small cloud disappeared. With their eyes moist with tears and their hearts filled with great joy, the people left the Cova, knowing that the Blessed Virgin had been faithful to her appointment.

Six days after the missed appointment, the Virgin appeared to Lucia, Francisco and Jacinta at a place called Valinhos. After having expressed her regret about those who had prevented the children from coming to meet her, she told them that as a result the miracle promised for October would not be as great. As always, she added, "Pray. Pray much and make sacrifices for sinners. Many souls go to hell because no one makes sacrifices for them." Then she disappeared.

By this time, no one doubted the sincerity of the three shepherds. On September 13, about 30,000 people gathered at the Cova.

"Get back now! Let them pass!" some men shouted as they struggled to open up a path for the children in the midst of the pressing crowd.

Preceded by the usual signs, the Virgin appeared. She urged the children to keep on reciting the rosary for the war to end and asked them to return on the thirteenth of the next month, promising to bring Saint Joseph and the Infant Jesus with her at that time.

"I was told to ask you for many things," Lucia confided to the Lady. "Some sick people wish to be cured."

"I will cure some people," the beautiful Lady answered, "but not others. In October I will perform a miracle so that everyone may believe."

## 11

# THE MIRACLE OF THE SUN

October 13, 1917, dawned cold and wet. The dirt roads were muddy from the heavy rain which had fallen without let-up throughout the night. Yet despite the rain, a constant stream of people poured into the Cova from all parts of Portugal.

Both the prayerful and the curious huddled beneath a forest of dripping umbrellas. The crowd of nearly 70,000 persons anxiously awaited the hour of the Virgin's apparition.

Around noon, Jacinta, Francisco, and Lucia arrived. They were dressed in their best clothes and carrying bouquets of flowers. The children were nearly crushed by the pressure of the crowd around them. This made Jacinta cry.

Lucia ordered the people to close their umbrellas. In spite of the fact that the rain was still coming down in torrents, the crowd immediately obeyed. Then Lucia started the rosary. At the sound of the noonday bells, she stopped.

"There she is! There she is!" she exclaimed. "I see her!" Lucia's face assumed a superhuman beauty and her lips became pale.

Francisco and Jacinta, too, were deep in ecstasy.

The crowd watched in silent awe. There, next to the holm oak tree, they saw a white cloud form about the seers, and rise up to a height of five or six yards. This happened three times.

"Dear Lady, who are you and what do you wish?" Lucia asked.

The radiant Lady answered, "I am the Lady of the Rosary. I desire that a chapel be built on this spot in my honor. Continue always to pray the rosary every day. I promise that if the people will change their lives, I will hear their prayers, and will bring the war to a speedy end. . . . I have come to tell people to ask forgiveness for their sins." The Virgin's beautiful face appeared very sad as she added, "Do not offend the Lord our God anymore, because he is already so much offended."

The Lady gazed tenderly upon the three children. She let them understand that this was the last time they would see her on earth. Then she gestured toward the heavens. Turning to see what the Lady was pointing at, Lucia impulsively cried out, "Look at the sun!" A great shout rose up from the crowd. An incredible spectacle, which was to last about twelve minutes, was about to begin. . . .

The rain abruptly stopped. The clouds rolled back, broke, and scattered, as if swept away by a mighty wind rising up from the earth. High above the horizon, the sun appeared. But instead of its usual blinding brilliance, it was a cool silvery-white color. The people were able to look directly into it without being blinded. As they watched, the sun began to spin like a large wheel of fire, shooting out shafts of yellow, red, green, violet, and blue light. Clouds, trees, mountains, and fields were fantastically colored by its rays. Even the faces of the stunned crowd reflected these colors.

Twice, for an instant or more, the sun stopped. Then the violent jerking and whirling began all over again, raining down light and countless streams of color.

In the meantime, the children alone saw, one after the other, four scenes acted out near the sun. While the Virgin Mary slowly rose to the right of the sun, Saint Joseph joined her at its left. He was holding the

Infant Jesus, who appeared as a child about a year old. The Virgin now wore a blue mantle over her white dress. Saint Joseph and Jesus were clothed in red. An instant later, this vision vanished. Now Jesus, as a grown man, stood at the base of the sun. He blessed the people and then disappeared. Next the children saw the Virgin appear as Our Lady of Sorrows, but without the sword piercing her heart. Finally Mary appeared as Our Lady of Mount Carmel, holding the brown scapular in her hand.

These visions ended just as the sun was about to repeat its swirling and dancing for the third and last time. Rotating with an ever-increasing speed, it tore itself from the sky and began a fiery plunge toward the earth. The people screamed in terror.

"Lord, have mercy on me!"

"My God! I believe in you!"

"Mary, help us!"

Many thought the end of the world had come. All over the field, men, women and children fell to their knees in the thick mud.

Then, just as suddenly as it had begun, the sun halted its wild downward race. It stopped spinning and returned to its usual position, taking on its normal color again. A great sigh of relief ran through the crowd.

*"A miracle! A miracle!"*

When the people had recovered their senses, they realized that their clothes, which had been drenched in the torrential downpour, were now completely dry!

The promised sign from heaven had come. "A miracle! A miracle!" the shout went up from the electrified crowd. "Praised be our Lady!"

And the spectacle hadn't been limited to the Cova da Iria. People for twenty to thirty miles around had also seen the miracle of the sun.

# 12

# "I Can't Bless"

Even after the apparitions were over, many curious people came to Fatima to search out the young shepherds and talk with them. The cousins developed a real genius for hiding. One day, for example, a car of well-dressed men and women pulled up as the children were walking down the road. "I think they're coming to look for us," Francisco whispered.

"Let's run away!" Jacinta suggested.

"No, they've seen us already. Just act normal and they won't even recognize us."

One of the passengers leaned out the window. "Do you know the three little shepherds to whom the Virgin appeared?"

"Yes, we know them," Francisco replied in a calm voice.

"Could you please tell us where they live?"

"Sure. Follow this road until it ends. Make a right and then a left. A little farther on you'll come to a house. That's where they live."

The visitors thanked him and sped off down the road.

On another afternoon, Mrs. Marto was worried. Francisco had been missing for several hours and couldn't be found. When Lucia and Jacinta came in, she asked them to look for him.

After Mrs. Marto had left the room, the girls heard a loud whisper. "Jacinta, Lucia, I'm up here!"

It was Francisco's voice, and it seemed to be coming from the ceiling! They looked up and saw him balancing on the rafters.

"What are you doing?" they giggled.

"There were so many people looking for us," he explained, as he started to climb down. "What could I have told them? I didn't hear the Virgin speak."

Francisco had a very sensitive heart and always tried to help those in any kind of need. There was an elderly woman in Fatima whom everyone called "Aunt Mary." Since she was partially paralyzed, she found it hard to round up her flock of sheep and goats. The animals usually ran off in all directions when she tried to call them. But whenever she saw Francisco, Aunt Mary was relieved. Francisco would race around the field to help the old woman gather her flock. Then, just as quickly, he would disappear without waiting to be thanked.

Francisco could also be very outspoken, in a kind but forceful way, in the face of evil.

One day he came across a woman who was surrounded by a large crowd. She was a fortuneteller and was pretending to bless religious articles. She made a good living from the money she charged for her "blessings."

When Francisco came closer, she asked him to bless some religious articles himself. "I can't bless," he answered quietly, "and neither can you. Only priests can give blessings." This put an end to the fortuneteller's booming business.

"We don't know what power Francisco has," people often remarked, "but when we're near him, we somehow feel that we ourselves are better."

His goodness was a reflection of his own love for Jesus and Mary.

One of the things that made Jacinta stand out was her special love for the Holy Father. One time, two priests came to question the children about the apparitions of the Virgin Mary. Before leaving, they asked Jacinta, Francisco and Lucia to pray for the Pope, because he needed many prayers. "Who is the Pope?" Jacinta innocently asked. The priests explained to her that the Pope, or the Holy Father as we also call him, is the successor of Saint Peter and represents Jesus in leading the Church here on earth. After that Jacinta always added the words "and for the Holy Father" when she offered a sacrifice to Jesus.

Even though Jacinta never got to meet the Pope in person, twice God allowed her to see a vision of Pope Pius XII, who was the Holy Father at that time. Once she told Lucia, "I don't know how it happened, but I saw the Holy Father in a big house. He was kneeling by a little table. He covered his face with his hands and prayed . . . and he was crying! Outside there were crowds of people. Some were throwing stones. Others were swearing and saying mean things about the Pope."

After this, Jacinta prayed even more for the Pope who had to lead the Church through a very difficult period of history.

## 13

# MARY COMES AGAIN

Months passed. World War I finally ended. The rattle of machine guns, the roar of cannons and the whistle of falling missiles were silenced. But their echo continued to ring in the homes of many grieving families. How many sons, husbands, and fathers had not come home from the war!

The war had claimed many victims, but Spanish influenza was taking even more. (At that time, many of the medicines that we have today were not available, and viruses spread quickly.) In December 1918, about a year after the last apparition, Francisco and Jacinta caught this form of the flu. It brought with it fever, muscular pain and infection and swelling of the respiratory tract. Would this be the illness that would bring them to heaven? They multiplied their sacrifices. Whenever Lucia visited her cousins' house, Jacinta would send her to go see Francisco as a little sacrifice. Francisco, in turn, would ask Lucia to do the same for Jacinta.

Although Francisco grew weaker day by day, his desire to offer God small sacrifices and acts of love seemed to be getting stronger.

"Are you suffering, Francisco?" Lucia asked him one day.

"Yes, very much. But I suffer everything for love of our Lord and of our Blessed Mother." He tried to smile, then added, "I wish I could suffer even more, Lucia, but honestly, I can't."

On some days he wasn't able to pray the entire rosary. Even though he had already prayed many, he felt that he still had many more to say.

"Mamma," he sadly confided, "I can't say the whole rosary anymore. When I get halfway through, my head just starts spinning...."

"Pray with your heart, then, Francisco," his mother encouraged him. "The Virgin will be pleased just the same."

One morning, Jacinta sent for Lucia. Lucia rushed to her cousins' house, wondering what had happened.

"Our Lady came to see us!" Jacinta excitedly explained. "She said she'll soon take Francisco with her to heaven. She asked me if I wanted to convert more sinners. I told her yes." Jacinta paused to take a breath, then hurried on. "The Virgin also told me that I'll go to the hospital. I'll suffer a lot there, but I should offer it all up for sinners, for the Holy Father, in reparation for the sins committed against her Immaculate Heart, and for the love of Jesus."

Francisco's sickness developed into bronchial pneumonia. On April 2, his condition became alarming, and he was running a very high fever.

"Papa," he said to his father, "I want to receive Holy Communion before I die."

"Of course you will," answered Mr. Marto in a trembling voice. "I'll go for the pastor right away."

Then Francisco sent for Lucia. She came immediately. "Lucia, I want to go to confession in order to receive Holy Communion before I die," Francisco said quietly. "Tell me if you ever saw me commit any sins."

Lucia thought for a minute. "Sometimes you disobeyed your mother and came to see me when she had told you to stay home," she honestly answered.

"Yes, that's true. Thank you. Now go and ask Jacinta if she remembers anything else."

Jacinta remembered that once, before the apparitions, Francisco had taken a few cents from his father to buy a harmonica, and also that with some other friends he had thrown stones at boys from Boleiros.

Lucia returned and reported what Jacinta had said. "I've already confessed those things," Francisco replied. "But I'll confess them again. Who knows how sad I made the Lord because of these sins? If I were to live, I wouldn't commit them again. Now I'm sorry." He lowered his head for a moment, then looked back up at his cousin.

"Lucia, you ask God to forgive me, too."

"I will," she answered, "but God loves you and has already forgiven you, Francisco. Remember, the Virgin said that she would soon come to take you to heaven. I'm going to Mass now, and I'll pray for you there."

"Listen," he pleaded, "ask Jesus to make our pastor bring me Holy Communion."

Lucia nodded.

## 14

# FRANCISCO GOES HOME

Francisco's last and greatest wish was to receive Jesus in the Holy Eucharist. (He had missed out on receiving his First Communion because he had had some trouble in stating one of the truths of the Apostles' Creed.)

The pastor came. He heard Francisco's confession, and promised to bring him Holy Communion the following day.

Francisco could hardly wait. When the priest finally returned, Francisco could no longer sit up in bed because of his extreme weakness.

That Holy Communion brought him deep joy. He could feel God within him just as he had when he and Jacinta drank from the angel's chalice almost three years earlier.

Later that day Francisco asked his family to forgive him for anything he had ever done to displease them.

"Say a rosary for me," he begged Jacinta and Lucia. "I can't pray anymore because of the pain."

"Are you still suffering a lot, Francisco?" they asked him when the rosary was ended.

"Enough, but it doesn't matter. I'm suffering to console Jesus. Anyway, soon I'll go to heaven."

He looked at Jacinta. He'd be seeing her soon.

He looked at Lucia. "I'm going to miss you, Lucia," he whispered. "If only the Virgin would call you to heaven soon, too!"

"Good-bye, Francisco!" Lucia murmured. "If you go to paradise tonight, don't forget me up there!"

"Don't worry. I'll never forget you!"

Taking her hand, he squeezed it tightly. Tears filled his eyes.

"Is there something else you want to say?" Lucia asked.

"No," Francisco answered in a choked voice.

The scene was becoming so emotional that Mrs. Marto asked Lucia and Jacinta to leave the room.

"Good-bye, then, Francisco, till we meet in heaven," said Lucia quietly.

"I'll be seeing you up there!" he answered.

Jacinta stayed a few minutes longer. She wanted Francisco to bring a message to heaven for her. "Tell Jesus and the Lady that

I greet them with all my love," she instructed. "Tell them that I'll suffer everything for the conversion of sinners who don't accept their love, and to make reparation to the Immaculate Heart of Mary."

Francisco nodded. A few moments later, he was fast asleep under the anxious gaze of his mother.

Bright sunlight poured through the bedroom window on the morning of April 4, 1919. Around 6:00 A.M., Francisco suddenly called out, "Mama! Mama!"

"What is it, Francisco? What do you need?"

Francisco's face was lit by a radiant smile and his arms were outstretched as if he were reaching for someone. "Look, Mama! There . . . near the door. . . . What a beautiful light! What a beautiful light!"

The Lady from heaven had come to take him home with her, just as she had promised.

## 15

# JACINTA LEAVES FOR HEAVEN

Jacinta's illness continued to worsen after Francisco's death. Soon she could hardly leave her bed. She was taken to the Hospital of Saint Augustine in Ourem, where she stayed for two full months. Seeing no improvement, the doctors finally sent her home.

Lucia often stopped to visit Jacinta on her way to school. One day Jacinta told her, "Listen, tell the hidden Jesus (her name for Jesus present in the Holy Eucharist) that I like him, that I love him very much!"

When she noticed her mother looking sad at seeing her suffer so much, Jacinta would say, "Don't worry, Mama. I'm going to heaven. There I'll pray hard for you."

After six months of battling the flu, Jacinta developed a severe case of pleurisy. The membrane surrounding her lungs became inflamed and she often suffered from a fever and coughing spells.

Although she was so sick, Jacinta continued to offer up small sacrifices to God. She got to the point where drinking even a little milk or broth was very difficult. Hoping to tempt her to eat something, her mother brought in a delicious bunch of grapes one day, along with a glass of milk. "If you can't drink the milk, Jacinta, at least have some grapes," she pleaded.

"I don't want the grapes, Mama. But I'll have the milk."

After Mrs. Marto left the room, Jacinta turned to Lucia. "I was dying to eat those grapes," she admitted, "and it was very hard for me to drink the milk. But I wanted to offer this sacrifice to our Lord."

The Blessed Virgin visited Jacinta one last time. Jacinta shared the Virgin's message with Lucia. "She told me that I'm going to go to another hospital, one in Lisbon. And I'm never going to see you or my parents again. After suffering a lot, I'm going to die alone." Jacinta's sad face suddenly brightened. "But, Lucia, the Blessed Virgin also said that she will come herself to take me to heaven!"

"And what will you do there in heaven?"

Jacinta broke into a big smile. "Oh, I'll love Jesus and Mary so much!" she cried excitedly. "And I'll ask them to help you, and the Holy Father, and my parents and

*"I'll never, ever see you again!"*

brothers and sisters, and everyone who's asked me to pray for them, and all sinners!"

Many times Lucia brought her little cousin flowers that she had picked near the Cova da Iria. One day, big tears rolled down Jacinta's cheeks as she took the flowers from Lucia. "I'm never going back to there again," she sobbed, "and I miss it so much!"

"What difference does it make," Lucia said softly as she dabbed at the tears with a handkerchief, "now that you're going to heaven to see our Lord and our Lady?"

"Oh, that's right," Jacinta smiled, as she began plucking off the petals to count them.

The day finally came for Jacinta to be taken to the Hospital of Dona Stefania in Lisbon, where she would undergo surgery to remove two infected ribs. Sobbing, she hugged Lucia tightly for a long time. "I'll never, ever see you again!" she cried. "You can't be with me, but pray for me, very much, until I go to heaven. Up there I'll remember you. Don't tell anybody the secret, even if they kill you for it. Love Jesus and the Immaculate Heart of Mary with all your heart. And make many sacrifices for sinners!"

At first Jacinta's surgery seemed to be successful, but soon her condition was worse than ever. She was in terrible pain. Sister

Mary, the superior of a nearby orphanage, came to visit her every day. Jacinta called her "Madrina," which means "little mother."

The Blessed Virgin came several times to visit Jacinta in the hospital, too. Arriving at her bedside one morning, Sister Mary was surprised when Jacinta exclaimed, "Please come back later, Madrina! I'm expecting the Lady now!"

On one of these visits, Mary let Jacinta know the exact day and hour when she would go to heaven. Four days before she died, all her pains suddenly disappeared and Jacinta experienced a great peace. On the night of Friday, February 20, 1920, she received the sacrament of Reconciliation and begged to receive Jesus in Holy Communion. Believing that she still had several hours to live, the priest did not bring her the Eucharist. That same night, at 10:30, the Blessed Virgin came to bring Jacinta to heaven, just as she had come for Francisco.

Lucia later became a Carmelite nun and worked to spread devotion to Mary's Immaculate Heart. Lucia died on February 13, 2005, at the age of ninety-seven.

On May 13, 2000, Jacinta and Francisco were beatified in Fatima. The miracle required for this beatification was the complete healing of Maria Emilia Santos, a woman who had been bedridden with tuberculosis for twenty years. Maria had prayed to God for healing through the intercession of Jacinta and Francisco. She was miraculously cured in 1987. After approval of another miracle, Jacinta and Francisco were canonized by Pope Francis on May 13, 2017.

Jacinta, who was almost ten years old when she died, and Francisco, who would have turned eleven in just two more months, are the youngest children the Catholic Church has ever honored as saints. We can ask them to pray for us and help us to love God and our Blessed Mother as they did. We can also ask them to remind us that there are still many people who don't love God and who offend him by their actions or words. Like Francisco and Jacinta, we can offer our prayers and acts of love and sacrifice to the Lord so that everyone will accept the love, mercy, and forgiveness God wants to give us.

## 16

# Fatima Today

In 1917, a twelve-foot high wooden arch was built over the spot where Mary had appeared to Lucia, Francisco and Jacinta. Two lanterns were hung on this simple marker. (The little holm oak tree on which our Lady had stood had been destroyed by *pilgrims* who took pieces from it as souvenirs.)

Construction work on a tiny chapel, called the *Chapel of the Apparitions*, began on August 6, 1918, the Feast of the Transfiguration. This chapel, still standing today, is so small that it can only hold about six people at a time.

In 1921, Bishop José da Silva, the bishop of Fatima at that time, decided to purchase thirty acres of land at the Cova da Iria. He wanted to set this land aside as a *shrine* to our Lady. He used donations given by pilgrims to buy the property. The next year, something terrible happened. During the night of March 6, 1922, some men bombed the Chapel of the Apparitions. The whole roof was destroyed, but the people immediately got to work and repaired it.

Today the chapel is also called the *Capelhina*, which means "little chapel" in Portuguese. A beautiful statue showing Mary as she appeared at the Cova da Iria stands on a pillar in front of the Capelhina. The statue and pillar mark the exact spot where Our Lady of Fatima appeared to the three young shepherds. José Ferreira Thedim, a famous Portuguese sculptor, carved the statue of our Lady from Brazilian cedar wood in 1920. It is painted in full color. Mary's hands are joined in prayer, and she holds a rosary. On the twelfth and thirteenth of the month from May to October, this statue of our Lady wears a special crown in honor of the *apparitions*. The lovely crown is a gift of the women of Portugal. It contains 313 pearls and 2,679 precious stones!

Right across from the Capelhina is the *Adoration Chapel*, where Jesus in the *Blessed Sacrament* is exposed day and night. Here pilgrims come to adore Jesus, to thank him, to ask for his help and to tell him they are sorry for their sins.

Nearby is a very large church called the *Basilica of Our Lady, Queen of the Holy Rosary*.

This is the "chapel" our Lady asked to have built in her honor. It was dedicated on the feast of Our Lady of the Rosary, October 7, 1953. On top of its 215-foot tower sits a bronze crown that weighs seven tons! Above the crown shines a large crystal cross. Inside the basilica are fifteen altars representing the fifteen *mysteries of the rosary*. The tombs of Jacinta and Francisco are in a side chapel of the basilica.

In the special *Chapel of Reconciliation* at the right of the basilica, pilgrims are invited to celebrate God's love and mercy in the wonderful sacrament of Penance or Reconciliation. Priests at this chapel hear confessions in many different languages. Here people from all over the world find the great joy and peace that comes from having their sins forgiven.

Every night, great crowds of pilgrims gather at the shrine of Our Lady of Fatima for the *candlelight procession* in which they carry lighted candles and walk together through the grounds praying and singing.

The largest groups of pilgrims—hundreds of thousands of them—come to Fatima on the thirteenth of each month from May to October. They do this in remembrance of the days on which the Blessed

Mother appeared to the children. As many as one million people attend the May celebrations at the shrine!

A tall *cross* at the entrance to the shrine greets pilgrims. It reminds them of the Blessed Virgin's invitation to us to *pray* and do *penance* for our own sins and for the sins of others. As an act of penance, some pilgrims cross the huge square in front of the basilica by walking on their knees. A long white path has even been set aside for people who wish to do this.

On the grounds of the shrine at Fatima there are also outdoor *Stations of the Cross*, representing Jesus on his way to his crucifixion on Mount Calvary. Many pilgrims pray the Stations, or Way of the Cross, to meditate on Jesus' sufferings, death and resurrection.

Not very far away, pilgrims can also visit the hill where the angel appeared to the children. This area is called the *Cabeço*. At the Cabeço are statues of Lucia, Francisco, Jacinta and the angel, who is holding a Host and a chalice.

Pilgrims visiting our Lady's shrine at Fatima today all share one thing in common—faith in God's love and care for them and trust in the special intercession and love of Mary. Sometimes, people who have visited Fatima and prayed there have been healed from their illnesses. But even people who don't receive a physical cure, go away with a new sense of peace and hope. This is Mary's special gift to them. It can be her special gift to you, too.

You may never be able to travel all the way to Portugal to visit her shrine, but you can live our Lady's message wherever you are, in your own small way. You can try to pray the rosary often—every day if possible—for peace in our world. You can receive the sacrament of Penance and Holy Communion on the first Saturday of each month in reparation for sins that offend God and the Immaculate Heart of Mary. You can also offer small acts of love and sacrifice to God to make up for people who refuse his love and mercy. You can try to do everything out of love for Jesus and Mary, just as Lucia, Francisco and Jacinta did. This is the best way to live and to spread the message of Our Lady of Fatima.

# PRAYER

*Saints Jacinta and Francisco, how wonderful it must have been to see Mary, the Mother of God!*

*It took a lot of courage for you to be her messengers, especially when people refused to believe you, or made fun of you.*

*Thank you for bringing us Mary's important message about prayer and penance, Jacinta and Francisco. Help me to pray for the peace that our world needs so badly. Help me to offer my own acts of love and sacrifice to make up in some small way for the sins that offend God and the Blessed Mother.*

*You are the two youngest children ever to be considered for sainthood. Remind me that even though I'm young, my love and my efforts to be like Jesus can make a real difference in the world. Please pray for me, Jacinta and Francisco.*

*Amen.*

# GLOSSARY

1. **Apparition**—someone or something that appears and is able to be seen by others.

2. **Beatification**—the ceremony in which the Pope, in the name of the Catholic Church, declares that a person lived a life of Gospel holiness in a heroic way. This is done after the person's life and holiness have been carefully researched. Beatification is the second step in the process of naming a person a saint. Canonization is when the Pope declares that somone is a saint in heaven.

3. **Blessed Sacrament**—another name for the Holy Eucharist, the real Body and Blood of the risen Jesus present under the appearances of bread and wine at Mass. The name Blessed Sacrament is especially used to refer to the Holy Eucharist kept, in the form of consecrated hosts, in the tabernacle.

4. **Conversion**—a change of heart.

5. **Ecstasy**—an experience in which the love of God is so strong inside a person that that person is temporarily not aware of what's going on around him or herself.

6. **Fasting**—going without food. By giving up food for a short time, a person offers God a sacrifice and shows that he or she depends only on him.

7. **Hamlet**—a small village.

8. **Intercession**—a type of prayer in which we ask God's help for a special favor. Jesus **intercedes** for us to God the Father. We can also pray to God through the intercession of Mary and the other saints.

9. **Penance**—a prayer or action that a person says or does to express his or her sorrow for sin.

10. **Pilgrims**—persons who travel to a holy place to pray and to feel closer to God. The journey they make is called a pilgrimage.

11. **Prostrate**—to lie face down or to bow very low.

12. **Purgatory**—a condition in which the souls of good persons who have died but are not yet ready to enter heaven are purified from the effects of their sins.

13. **Reparation**—the act of making up for a wrong or an injury. At Fatima, Our Lady asked the three children to make reparation for sins.

14. **Sacrifice**—anything that we give up to offer to God as a gift.

15. **Sacrilege**—the mistreatment of a person, place, or thing consecrated to God and his service.

16. **Shrine**—a holy place. A shrine is usually a place to which people go on pilgrimage to pray and to show their devotion to God, Mary, or one of the saints.

17. **Unrepentant**—not sorry.

# The Saints
## Pray for Us

For over two thousand years holy men and women have followed Jesus with amazing dedication, courage, and creativity. This beautifully illustrated book guides you in asking the saints to pray for you!

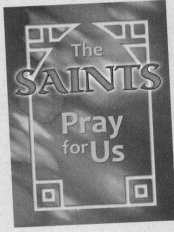

# Bible for
## Young Catholics

Every book of the Old and
New Testaments comes to
life through the pages of this
book with colorful illustrations,
maps, and historical notes.

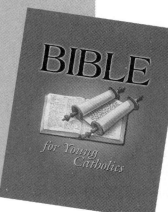

# Prayers for
## Young Catholics

This book of basic and more
advanced prayers, beautifully
expressed through interior
artwork, explains the importance
of prayer and provides instruction
on how to pray.

![Pauline KIDS logo]

# Who are the Daughters of St. Paul?

We are Catholic sisters with a mission. Our task is to bring the love of Jesus to everyone like Saint Paul did. You can find us in over 50 countries. Our founder, Blessed James Alberione, showed us how to reach out to the world through the media. That's why we publish books, make movies and apps, record music, broadcast on radio, perform concerts, help people at our bookstores, visit parishes, host JClub book fairs, use social media and the Internet, and pray for all of you.

**Visit our Web site at www.pauline.org**

## BOOKS & MEDIA

The Daughters of St. Paul operate book and media centers at the following addresses. Visit, call, or write the one nearest you today, or find us at www.paulinestore.org.

**CALIFORNIA**
3908 Sepulveda Blvd, Culver City, CA 90230 — 310-397-8676
3250 Middlefield Road, Menlo Park, CA 94025 — 650-369-4230

**FLORIDA**
145 S.W. 107th Avenue, Miami, FL 33174 — 305-559-6715

**HAWAII**
1143 Bishop Street, Honolulu, HI 96813 — 808-521-2731

**ILLINOIS**
172 North Michigan Avenue, Chicago, IL 60601 — 312-346-4228

**LOUISIANA**
4403 Veterans Memorial Blvd, Metairie, LA 70006 — 504-887-7631

**MASSACHUSETTS**
885 Providence Hwy, Dedham, MA 02026 — 781-326-5385

**MISSOURI**
9804 Watson Road, St. Louis, MO 63126 — 314-965-3512

**NEW YORK**
115 E. 29th Street, New York City, NY 10016 — 212-754-1110

**SOUTH CAROLINA**
243 King Street, Charleston, SC 29401 — 843-577-0175

**TEXAS**
Currently no book center; for parish exhibits or outreach evangelization, contact: 210-569-0500, or SanAntonio@paulinemedia.com, or P.O. Box 761416, San Antonio, TX 78245

**VIRGINIA**
1025 King Street, Alexandria, VA 22314 — 703-549-3806

**CANADA**
3022 Dufferin Street, Toronto, ON M6B 3T5 — 416-781-9131

¡También somos su fuente para libros, videos y música en español!